The Brittle Gods
::
Ancient Themes
Rethought

The Brittle Gods
::
Ancient Themes Rethought

Poems by Terence Kuch

Apprentice House Press
Loyola University Maryland

First Edition

Paperback ISBN: 978-1-62720-179-7
E-book ISBN: 978-1-62720-180-3

Printed in the United States of America

Design by Paul Volante
Marketing by Caroline Cox
Development by Carmen Machalek

Published by Apprentice House

Apprentice House
Loyola University Maryland
4501 N. Charles Street
Baltimore, MD 21210
410.617.5265 • 410.617.2198 (fax)
www.apprenticehouse.com
info@apprenticehouse.com

... the square glass altars
where the brittle gods are kept,
the relics of what we have destroyed,
our holy and obsolete symbols.
— Margaret Atwood

Contents

Foreword

by Susan Notar

Everything old is new again in these poems by Terence Kuch. In his afterword he notes that he found the inspiration for these pieces while on a visit to Thebes and other parts of Greece when he experienced the ancient and modern worlds colliding, And what a collision it is!

The reader will find gods and people both famous and less well known in Kuch's work, including Apollo, Oedipus, Eros, Cassandra, and many others. Readers may be inspired to discover more about these gods and heroes of ancient times.

Better known gods do appear, such as Dionysos, and subject matter too, for there is much feasting, and loving, and war. Funny, it sounds like our modern era.

There are spare poems that you may be tempted to taste one at a time like a perfect globed grape, or all at once in a lavish feast of words. Some are humorous, such as "The Singer," while others are mournful, such as "The Day We Lost," about the defeat of the Spartan army. Still others are erotic, such as "Anamnesis," describing two lovers who have kissed or who are about to.

In many places the language is startlingly beautiful and unexpected such as in "On Delos was bright Apollo born," where the first stanza reads "the sea off Delos flashed like / trampled glass / each breaker caught / in brilliant air."

A common theme among these poems is the implicit invitation to slow own. To stop our incessant textingemailposting and linger. Enjoy.

> Susan Notar is a poet living in Northern Virginia whose work has appeared in a number of publications including *Joys of the Table, An Anthology of Culinary Verse.*

The Gate of Hell

"Gate of Hell" they tell the tourists,

but what a fake!
Yes, there's a hole in the ground,
a rotting iron grate,
a lock – a child could break.

Tourists gape, grab a shot
then the bus goes on to Aulis,
Delphi, some other place.

Last bus gone for the day,
keepers sweep up butts and paper cups,
truck up the blood, tip the barrel,
pour it fresh and hot through the grate.

Hell's broken souls
mew and scramble like cats,
shoving and pushing
then finally sated they glow with repast,
tell stories of when they were live,

where they went,

what they saw.

The Hungry Gods

On holy days we go to the Tower to present our offerings of meat and grain, ask the gods for rain, fertile wives, grateful children.

Sometimes the gods grant our prayers; often they do not.

A few scoffers say there are no gods in the Tower, or anywhere else; if our prayers are answered it is just by chance.

But they can't explain why our offerings have disappeared by the next morning. And not just the food, but the bowls and cups and knives as well. And sometimes the priests, too, just a few bloodstains...

"On Delos was bright Apollo born"

The sea off Delos flashed like
trampled glass
each breaker caught
in brilliant air

And then
a liturgy of slivered light –

Now the god is born

An Ancient Contract

We agree to pay Kleanthos
ten plates of meat
from the civic feast
and not all the worst parts,
or deer found rotting in the hills.

And we agree to pay him
fifty jugs of wine
put up in harvest
(but ten in a bad year)

to be memory among us
when our old men forget.

Recall the battles of our gods,
their lineage and strength!
Relate our deeds of war and wealth
and tell our daughters' freshness
to our listening eyes.

We inscribe our names below
(some of us with doubts)
but if Kleanthos agrees
to do these things, and fails,
may his daughters die before his eyes
and may he remember the sight

forever.

"There he is..."

There he is, old Anacreon,
butt of jokes and pranksters,
one shoe gone, song off-key,
his lover somewhere
else with someone else.

Father Dion keep him safe;
save his soul from –
boredom!

Dionysos in Aulis

Here's a shot, blue guides and green guides agree,
a photo place, family squinting up at the Attraction,
backs against a dark park service sign, stop teasing
your sister now, hold still just one more time.

Then turning right on forty-four, just past a pier
where still ships wait for wind, *Look!* up to your left
there it is: the shrine great Dion built to honor
and amuse himself, twined ivy and vines,
shredded light through leaves.

Stop the car and enter in quite hushed
not sure if this place is a church, or what.

                                    There he stands,
the god in warm white stone carved in swaggering stride,
thick pouting, curling lips and hooded eyes that urge
Partake; Forget.

– But we passed the place by, content with dry
description, not turning right on forty-four
but holding the wheel very tight, staring
straight down the road remembering another time,
when sails hung loose days after weeks,
impatient generals sharing nods.
                              We did

       . . . .

what we had to, then slapped our shields
on swaying hulls for luck, sails snapping like dogs.

Here's a bright-colored card to honor the god,
a letter filled with doings of the year,
pictures of Cimmeria,

signs.

For Demetrios

They say no one has been killed
by the sweet forbearing god,
never mind the shaking angry sky above
or tyrant's crushing rule below.

No one but Demetrios –
But no, they say, only
one of his thieving guards,
splayed bleating on the altarstone,
pressed down hard
by some invisible hand
until his various moistures
leaked like rotten fruit.

They say the sweet avenging god
has left you for last,
Demetrios!

The Gift

It is easier to raise a shrine than bring the deity down to haunt it. – Samuel Beckett

After taxes
that pre-humbled our people
for practice,

After importing marble
at great cost and fighting off tribes
to bring it here,

And after many crushed limbs
in the building of it
and the spiremaker's falling-death –

      We built the shrine.

Even from the day
of cornerstone and speech

The gods were there among us
shouting, boistering,
cajoling the stonemasons on,

Eager for the altar's gift
to fill their brimming lips.

"I took the garland"

I took the garland from
his withered head
and placed it on my own.
Fool I was! Now Eros has me
captive in his hand.

Seeing

Let us see / Where we have come. – Oedipus at Colonus

Tall clouds stand overhead high on Cithaeron
this fortieth day of shadowed light, air heavy
and warm on the ground, a noontime eclipse.
Sodden rot of pallid grass lies on the bones of the land;
leaves curl and clutch like claws of dead birds.

Wild bulls stamp and snort, the hills' far noise,
saying simple things of cows and grass
and what is theirs. I hear again Tiresias tell my
recusant mind I killed my father: simple fact.

Long blades of grass lie across the sopping earth,
this rough cart-way to Colonus, stacked on edge
or knocked awry where travelers strayed before
or some beast lay to pass a hidden afternoon.

                                        And yet
my halting foot feels fresh life rising from the
squelching ground, sharp shoots thrusting up,
new life since my eyes bought away the curse.

                                        And now
the road slopes down to a place and its ever-
officious king, glad to reign in some small town
whose people still believe in the gods.

                        : :

It was she who saw them first. The rest turned back and
would not look, the city and its old family I loved to death.

I held the ornamented pins and watched them come
toward
my eyes, not to have those golden scalpels my last sight,
no,
I would have had Jocasta's still-warm breasts to look at
last,
but I had to see the pins to guide them home.

These were designs that lay against her skin
before my love's white gown, now held unclasped,
brushed soft nipples and fell away around her waist:

Designs worked in gold, worn from Jocasta's hands
and my hands and the hands of my father.
On the outside, graceful women holding urns;
inside, roughly wrought, the gods, their
anger, laughter, scorn, their wrenching roaring
WRATH.

Antigone saw them first, my unpierced eyelids
and what they told of what I saw
at last.

My Own Business

There I was
minding my own business
just lying there
on the anvil
speaking of nothing in particular
when Eros
slammed me with his hammer,
speechless.

Where ... ?

Where do the multitude of Gods dwell? – Cicero

We looked here and there: in the clouds, in the earth we thumped hoping to hear an answering sound, or feel soft shaking; but there was no response.

And when the earthen gods did consent to shake and topple the temples of the sky gods, it was not at our bidding nor at the place where we sacrifice our bleating lambs to them.

Truly, the ways of the gods are beyond us mere mortals. Just in case, however, we have taken up praying.

It is some comfort in the silence.

Deo Volente

Thy will be done – thy will!
The nodding, cunning gods,
we thought they wanted prayer from us,
and maybe even Love –

But no, but that was all for show.
They wanted our souls —
to gorge on.

The Temple Statue Speaks

I am not a likeness of the god,
I *am* the god.
If not me, then where is it?
Let the god for once show itself!

Four Oracles :: I

Gods cheat.

Be careful when you ask them "If..."
"If I avenge myself on Amphion..."
"If I indulge my whim for Theron's flesh..."

Gods cheat:

they do not know this "If–"; the gods
will make them Be, these "If's":

Amphion lying dead
                    by unknown hand,
sweet Theron
            trailing you from place to place
long after you've tired of him –

"O I can see the future!" is easy
enough for them to say:
                            they're gods.

Watch your wallet at the holy place.

Four Oracles :: II

I have brought you oxen-flesh
spiced with capers and peppercorns,
O god of this place, to please
your holy hunger.
                I have bought
and slain the red-beribboned lamb
and heard your bright-robed specialists proclaim
what its soft plumbing tells:

                        That I
may now descend into this rank and dripping
cave to beg you:

           Let the past turn out
           a different way
                    for me.

I have brought you rich meats if you
will not be bought with gold; but if you will,
I have brought that practical metal,

                      too.

Four Oracles :: III

See the parking lot? We used
to fill it every day, priestess girls
around the clock, three shifts.

                              Ah,

the wafting smoke of sacrifice and
vital questions of the day! "How fill
the sails of Agamemnon's ships?"
"What cure for Thebes from hateful
plague?"

                    But now – !

All we hear is "What's my lucky
number?"; "Will Pylos pay me back?";
"Who was that hunk from Hybla? Will I
lie with him again?"

                    And not a lot

of even that. We do the best we can
with what we've got, girls gone
flabby and grey, recruiting's
not so good, we can't afford
the going rate.

                              What

to do?

What

to do?

Four Oracles :: IV

At Ptoüs there was an oracle that never lied. – Pausanias

Now that you have asked
and slain the garlanded ox,
wrapped its thighbones
and heaven's nose has caught
the scent of sweetfired fat

Now that you have asked, I wreathe
the sacred mist about myself
and see a line of running, shouting
bronze-greaved men eight-deep
and say what we would have you know:

"Your great proud-pointed spear shall hear acclaim!"

    I do not say the words
    the god and I might say:

"An enemy will seize your spear and use it well."

Then Greeks will raise their widened eyes and smite their
foreheads
hard and say

"the god, again!

(that clever

god)"

An Ancient Decree About Maps

On any map of our kingdom
the chamberlain cares to have made

our capital must take up
all the space,
even to the folds and curls,

    And likewise

on maps of our capital
the palace grounds must
only be shown,

    And even there

only the temple,
the innermost temple,
the idol's porch,
the grand beast itself,
its glowing eyes;

only the darkness

in its glowing eyes.

Corpse

When a man died in archaic Greece, his wife was compelled to spend one night with the corpse, to ease its passage to the next world.

Many of these women remembered, the rest of their lives, their marriage to a cold unfeeling man.

The Honored Prophet Speaks

I am revered; every word cherished,
etched in gold or set in stone.

The people say: my words have come
from the spewing mouth of God.

I do not remember this,
but I suppose it might be so.

I am distressed that they honor
God's words, not my own.

Surely *I* have something to say.

– Don't I?

A Lover's Prayer

Why am I praying up
to bright Apollo,
sun-blind in the light?

Because the lusty gods
I prayed to
didn't turn that young man's
love to me;
and so at last I'm trying

Reason!

The Gods Come to Lystra

And when the people saw what Paul had done, they lifted up their voices, saying in the speech of Lycaonia, "The gods are come down to us in the likeness of men!" — Acts 14:11

Hermes came to our town today –
with Zeus! We knew them well from their
disguise and voice: the speech of Greece,
the dusty robes of men who foot

the rutted road to this poor place,
a god-forgotten Legion's post,
an almost nameless place upon
a high and treeless, rainless plain.

They came to test or please us; Zeus,
perhaps, to pour himself as rain
or gold into a village bride
and get a blessed child upon her.

A word from Zeus and old Lucullus
stood and walked, leaped a lifetime's
shake to steady out, as firm as bone.
We knew for sure then who they were,

Hermes of the rock-pile cairns,
sky god's guide, and Zeus the god
of gods himself, skybolt-thrusting
lord of thunder, lord of cloud.

They spoke inside the village gate
in Greek; their passion's fire made up
our lack of heaven's tongue.
They told us of the gods' demands and threats,

of how they come to man as men,
of life and death and life again.
And how they looked? Of Hermes, first,
or "Paul": a little man, his forehead

high, dark eyes deep set. His hands
and forearms shaped his words and smoothed
them out, rough arms thick and strong
and swept with curling streams of hair.

Then "Barnabas," or Zeus: behind
his herald, pale and tall, he watched
our village brides with eager care
to choose the one his bolt would bless.

They spoke again inside the gate,
and as they did we brought two oxen
and the wooden fillet garlands
for their horns. The oxen pranced

and pawed and when we led them up
to Zeus, one saw them bow their knees
toward the gods or thought he saw,
too quick for memory to catch.

The two saw our desire and raged
in hunger for the holy gift.
Then Hermes raised his arms and Zeus
called down his storm; they said as best

we heard "We are the passioned gods
of sky and earth, not men like you — ";
the oxen shook their horns in fright,
ran prancing, pawing, from the gate.

Then Zeus and Hermes motioned us
to follow them, and led us to
a feeble stream without a name
and taught us there a rite of Zeus'

and Hera's newest son and bade
us do it once to each. And then
they turned and blessed the place, and walked
away along the rutted road.

We swear to do this holy thing
until they send another son.
We watch for signs upon the village
brides; and feast on oxen bones.

Dixit

The god has spoken
old doubts gone

First water
trickles
spring hills

 New doubts

Hymn to Attis

I will hymn thee, Attis, Bright-one! Not quivering
to buzzing sounds as priests of Bacchus do,
or humming loudly through the nose in time to gut-string
twang
as Manicheans do;

but all in tune and metered time for Thee
in high clear tones. And I will mingle with the hymn
Idean music of the harp, the sound of pipes in almond
trees,
the roll of chant like river running
   All for Thee, O Attis, High-one!

I will hymn thee, Attis, Bright-one! Not calling thee
Bacchus or Pan or Adonis as others do,
or nameless All as sophists do,
or Christ as slaves and servants do,
   O Attis, High-one!

– after Hippolytus

Worthy of Statues

Statues scrape into the council chamber
    on their stone feet,

Speak the language of long ago,
    that far-gone age when
    gods were worthy of statues....

Cassandra

There he goes
sandals click-click
the marble-jointed
palace floor

Rigid tongue
dams my words
let him get it
wrong himself

Just two more steps
the gods' curse uncursed

———

Some thrashing tongue
whips mouth to speech

I call;
he turns

Circus Minimis

Train a god?
What kind of
omnipotent
Being would put up with
that?

Watch the eyes
old yellow-fang
squats and shifts his tub-top
rump

Swing the whip!

The God's New Statue

The rulers decapitated some other god's statue and put my stone head on it instead.

"Economy, you know," they said, "and besides, who remembers that old fart whose head is now in some museum basement, tipped over on its ear?"

But my new body did not like me. At night it shook, just a little because it was only stone, trying to dislodge its newfound head.

Be patient, I told it; I was only there until a more timely god came along, one more suited to the public's fickle taste.

I try to enjoy the time I have.

On Delos

One said,
Apollo was not born here
on Delos,
but somewhere else:
Paros, perhaps,
or Naxos.

We must make sure
One says this no more:

Loud gold-giving pilgrims hear,

bright Apollo's shrine

dim

Anamnesis

Long ago a god
decreed –

doddering, distracted, barely
recalling –

decreed that you and I would be here,

this night,

our searing lips

Another Song

*["I will remember you, Aphrodite, and another song also." –
The Homeric Hymns]*

He remembers their song

long after he forgets her –

but she, him.

One!

Count all my loves?
Can you number
leaves on the trees
or waves of the sea?

But I, in Eros' laughing
grasp, I count each lover
"One!"

The Day We Lost

The day we lost at Leuctra
we shame-dragged home

Cold Lysander
(thank the gods!)
his burning eyes

turned away

*[In 371 BC/BCE Thebes, avenging an earlier defeat by Lysander's
Spartans, crushed the Spartan army. The statue of Lysander at
Delphi was said to have crumbled, collapsed, or turned its back not to
witness the retreat of its defeated army. - TK]*

Solon in Egypt

"You Greeks!" he said,
genealogy still wet on my lips,
all sixteen generations back
and then a god.

Contempt and worse,
indulgence:
"Come with me," he said.
Down temple-steps, in tunnels
I stumbled on and just when
hard breathing came back late
he lit a torch. I saw
a cave, rows of dead men
wrapped in cloth.

           We walked,
he named them each
and then a sharp-stoned wall
with nothing left but all of earth.

"One hundred forty fathers' sons,"
he said,
"and still no god."

Thebes :: The Coming of War

Tearfully they bought keepsakes to send home ... in the event of their deaths. – Seven Against Thebes

Here under the power lines
beside the ruined quag
is a shrine about as wide
as a mailbox; peaked roof, glass-
paned walls, a few drachmas,
candle on a flat dish,
a prayer copied out by hand.

Something must have happened here
by the road under the power lines,
here where trucks rush on to Athens.

Perhaps it has to do with
the drive-in over there
where men of Argos are drinking
wine, buying postcards, edging
spears, making plans
          for Thebes.

Thebes :: The Harvest of War

And there shall not follow him any hands / pouring earth to make a tomb. – Seven Against Thebes

Ditches clog with rotting silt,
mottled mandarines bring coins
from hard-edged women.

Old men sit under the greying sky
like clothes spread out to dry
and here at the seventh gate lies
Polyneices, a spear through his neck.

Out on the marsh a young girl
digs a grave, wet sides
falling in as she bends.

The walls of Thebes are mostly down,
now; the king moved on to Livadea,
a place that always seems run down
but never really old. Creon says it's less
in danger from the tragic muse.

In the Gypsy camp they shake their heads
at the goings-on

               of Greeks.

The Singer

Not least among the noble hearts
for whom we heap up wreaths,
Anacreon, we honor you:
may you learn at last to smite the lyre
better than you did in life;
may you sing in tune at last;
may the flowered garland in your hair
be ever-fresh, and come to that,
may your hair — not leave next time
before the rest of you!

Acknowledgements

The "Oracle" poems were finalists for the annual award in poetry of the Dallas Poets Community, and were read by the author at the Community's annual reading at the McKinney Avenue Contemporary Theatre ("The Mac") in Dallas.

"The Day We Lost," "On Delos," and "Solon in Egypt" were originally published in *Copperfield Review*.

"On Delos Was Bright Apollo Born" was originally published in *Eternal Haunted Summer*.

"A Lover's Prayer" was originally published in the anthology *With Lyre and Bow*, Bibliotheca Alexandrina, 2016, under the title "Reason."

"Thebes – The Coming of War" was originally published in the anthology *Descansos: Words from the Wayside*, Darkhouse Books, 2017, and was nominated for a Pushcart Prize.

Sincere thanks to Meg Eden for her acute comments on these poems.

A Final Word

It was on a visit to Thebes that ancient and modern Greece suddenly collided for me: Trucks speeding their way to Colonus on roads where blind Oedipus once groped onward; radio towers shouting the latest oracle; *thetes* crowding Athens' Moschatou subway station between the long gone Long Walls.

It was all there, all at once – all that time: the air the earth the sea the stones; what Sophocles told us about a place comfortably far from town; what Pausanias that wonderful tourist saw and half-believed; what Byzantines and Turks, Romans and Roma, and many others saw in this brown place: that the old gods may have abandoned Antony but never, quite, abandoned Greece.

ἐμοί μέν οὖν λέγειν μέν τά ὑπό Ἑλλήνων λεγόμενα ἀνάγκη, πείθεσαι δέ πᾶσιν οὐκέτι ἀνάγκη. – Pausanias of Sardis (160 AD/CE)

("I am obliged to report what the Greeks tell me, but I am not obliged to believe them.")

Ω

About the Author

Terence Kuch was raised in the Cascade Mountains of Washington State. After jobs as a logger and postman, he graduated from Reed College in Portland, Oregon with a degree in philosophy, and later studied at the Corcoran School of Art, Johns Hopkins University, American University (M.S.), and Virginia Tech (Certificate in Advanced Graduate Study).

Terence Kuch's poetry, fiction, and non-fiction has been published in the U.S., U.K., Canada, Ireland, Australia, Luxembourg, and Thailand, including *Commonweal, Diagram, Dissent, Gravel, Grub Street, Luxembourg Review, Mademoiselle, The Moth, New Scientist, North American Review, Poetry Motel, Sheepshead Review, Thema, Timber Creek Review, Washington Post Book World, Washington Post Magazine, Yellow Mama,* and others. His novel, *The Seventh Effect,* was praised by Kirkus Reviews. A satirical poem of his won first prize in a New York magazine competition, was praised and reprinted in the *New York Times,* and included in a Random House-published collection. He studied at the Writers Center, Bethesda, Maryland, and participated in the Mid-American Review Summer Fiction Workshop. He has survived interviews by the *New York Times* (on I.T. for consumers) and USA Today (on 20th-century fiction). He lives in Springfield, Virginia, with a wife and several opinionated cats.

Apprentice House Press

Loyola University Maryland

Apprentice House is the country's only campus-based, student-staffed book publishing company. Directed by professors and industry professionals, it is a nonprofit activity of the Communication Department at Loyola University Maryland.

Using state-of-the-art technology and an experiential learning model of education, Apprentice House publishes books in untraditional ways. This dual responsibility as publishers and educators creates an unprecedented collaborative environment among faculty and students, while teaching tomorrow's editors, designers, and marketers.

Outside of class, progress on book projects is carried forth by the AH Book Publishing Club, a co-curricular campus organization supported by Loyola University Maryland's Office of Student Activities.

Eclectic and provocative, Apprentice House titles intend to entertain as well as spark dialogue on a variety of topics. Financial contributions to sustain the press's work are welcomed. Contributions are tax deductible to the fullest extent allowed by the IRS.

To learn more about Apprentice House books or to obtain submission guidelines, please visit www.apprenticehouse.com.

Apprentice House
Communication Department
Loyola University Maryland
4501 N. Charles Street
Baltimore, MD 21210
Ph: 410-617-5265 • Fax: 410-617-2198
info@apprenticehouse.com • www.apprenticehouse.com